RUBANK EDUCATIONAL LIBRARY No. 198

T0082071

Soloist Folio

FOR

C FLUTE with Piano Accompaniment

Compiled and Edited by Himie Voxman

CONTENTS

RUBANK®

HAL•LEONARD® CORPORATION

7777 W. BLUEMOUND RD. P.O. BOX 13819 MILWAUKEE, WI 53213

First Waltz

A. GRETCHANINOFF
Transcribed by H. Voxman

4

Little Berceuse
(Wiegenliedchen)

R. SCHUMANN, Op. 124, No. 6
Transcribed by H. Voxman

Menuetto
from Eine Kleine Nachtmusik

W. A. MOZART
Transcribed by H. Voxman

TRIO

p sotto voce

p

f

f

p sotto voce

p

(Solo part D.C.
written out)

Menuetto D.C. al Fine
(without repeats)

Barcarole

ERNESTO KÖHLER, Op. 30, No. 3
Edited by H. Voxman

Sarabanda and Rigaudon

I – SARABANDA

ARCANGELO CORELLI
Transcribed by H. Voxman

II-RIGAUDON

G. F. HANDEL
Transcribed by H. Voxman

poco rit. on repeat

poco rit. on repeat

Two Menuettos
from Flute Sonata in C

J. S. BACH
Edited by H. Voxman

II

Rondo - Finale

HAYDN-POPP
Edited by h. Voxman

The Swan
(Le Cygne)

CAMILLE SAINT-SAËNS
Transcribed by H. Voxman

RUBANK EDUCATIONAL LIBRARY No. 198

Soloist Folio

FOR

C FLUTE with Piano Accompaniment

Compiled and Edited by Himie Voxman

CONTENTS

●

HAL•LEONARD CORPORATION

7777 W. BLUEMOUND RD. P.O. BOX 13819 MILWAUKEE, WI 53213

First Waltz

C Flute

A. GRETCHANINOFF
Transcribed by H. Voxman

Little Berceuse
(Wiegenliedchen)

C Flute

R. SCHUMANN, Op. 124, No. 6
Transcribed by H. Voxman

Menuetto

from Eine Kleine Nachtmusik

C Flute

W. A. MOZART
Transcribed by H. Voxman

Barcarole

C Flute

ERNESTO KÖHLER, Op. 30, No. 3
Edited by H. Voxman

Sarabanda and Rigaudon

C Flute

I – SARABANDA

ARCANGELO CORELLI
Transcribed by H. Voxman

II – RIGAUDON

G. F. HANDEL
Transcribed by H. Voxman

poco rit. on repeat

Two Menuettos
from Flute Sonata in C

C Flute

I

J. S. BACH
Edited by H. Voxman

II

Rondo - Finale

C Flute

HAYDN-POPP
Edited by H. Voxman

The Swan
(Le Cygne)

C Flute

CAMILLE SAINT-SAËNS
Transcribed by H. Voxman

Musetta's Waltz Song
from La Bohème

C Flute

GIACOMO PUCCINI
Transcribed by H. Voxman

Bourrée and Menuet

from Flute Sonata No. III

C Flute

G. F. HANDEL
Edited by H. Voxman

Menuet
from Platée

C Flute

J. P. RAMEAU
Transcribed by H. Voxman

Waltz in F

C Flute

DANIEL STEIBELT
Transcribed by H. Voxman

Reverie

C Flute

CLAUDE DEBUSSY
Transcribed by Paul Koepke

Gavotte
from Paris and Helen

C. W. von GLUCK
Transcribed by H. Voxman

Andante

C Flute

RICHARD HERVIG

Musetta's Waltz Song
from La Bohème

GIACOMO PUCCINI
Transcribed by H. Voxman

Bourrée and Menuet
from Flute Sonata No. III

G. F. HANDEL
Edited by H. Voxman

Menuet
from Platée

J. P. RAMEAU
Transcribed by H. Voxman

D. C. al Fine
(without repeat)
2028-2

Waltz in F

DANIEL STEIBELT
Transcribed by H. Voxman

Reverie

CLAUDE DEBUSSY
Transcribed by Paul Koepke

Gavotte
from Paris and Helen

C. W. von GLUCK
Transcribed by H. Voxman

Andante

RICHARD HERVIG